The Fool's Book

The Fool's Book

John Danen

Published by John Danen, 2023.

THE FOOL'S BOOK

First edition. January 24, 2023.

ISBN: 979-8215267554

Written by John Danen.

Table of Contents

To the fools

Follow me on :

John Danen seduction - YouTube
John Danen seduction | Groups | Facebook
@johndanenseduccion - Instagram photos and videos.

Introduction.

The Fool's Book is a small humorous guide about the comportment of some subjects to avoid, so-called fools. It is related to the field of seduction in particular and in general to life. The fools exist, they are a threat and they must be eliminated at the root to succeed.

Unequivocal signs of foolishness.

If you are successful, it will not be long before strange phenomena manifest themselves that must be avoided and nullified at the root. These phenomena are emitted by male and sometimes also female subjects. The so-called fools.

The fool cannot accept that someone is better than he is at something and thus his envy arises. This envy will make the fool always do what can harm you the most because he wants to see you down like him. Come on! Let's see if fools appear, it is a sign of success. So the more and more burned they are, the better.

If you feel rejected, if you feel uncomfortable, or notice that you are not well-valued, it is that you have a fool attached to you. He is like a shark, a parasite. He contributes nothing and steals everything he can. Since he has nothing, not even hope, the only thing he has left is criticism. There he feels comfortable criticizing and belittling the successes of others.

Actions of a fool.

He refuses to go out.
- He refuses to go out and then you see him with other fools.
- Criticizes you behind your back.
- Withholds information that interests you.
- Doesn't help you when you need it.
- Belittles your successes.
- Overestimates yours, if they exist.
- Never congratulate you for anything.
- Refuses to believe things you tell him.
- I said you're a ghost.
- Tries to take away your morale.
- He's bland.
- He tells tasteless jokes in the presence of women.
- He makes you dependent on him and leaves you hanging.
- He lives optimistically in his world of failure.
- He never thinks of anything interesting.
- He looks at women's cleavage and terrifies them.
- He dances around making a fool of himself.
- Does not respect personal spaces and harasses.
- He has no sexual or love experience, or the one he has is ridiculous.
- Believes that others are like him.
- Drives badly and slowly.
- Has no magnetism whatsoever.
- He finds it difficult to relate to others.

- He harasses the girlfriends of his friends because he is incapable of approaching the girls.
- He loses his ass for the girls.
- Idolizes his girlfriend if he has one.
- He usually has a girlfriend of nimble beauty who dominates him.
- When he goes out, he leaves early.
- The girls use him and he does not realize it.
- He tries to waste his time in strange places where there are no possibilities.
- He doesn't know how to withdraw in time when entering a girl.
- He does not realize when a girl does not pay attention to him.
- He does not know how to materialize his opportunities.
- He goes in for horrible girls.
- He wastes his time talking about serious things.
- He'll go for anyone.
- He sometimes turns down good options because of prejudices.
- He asks you about your girlfriend when you are flirting.
- Thinks he has options with girls who hate him.
- He thinks he knows more than you.
- He never compliments.
- He has no friends, no girlfriend, no prospects.
- He cries for girls and does not recognize it.
- He resents girls.
- Some become completely demoralized.
- Others marry early and look fifteen years older than their age.
- Minimizes the length, intensity, and beauty of your girlfriends.
- Hint at supposed non-existent successes.
- Some are pedantic, some are shy, and some are insecure.
- Disdain anything that might help you flirt, such as books.
- Many are vulgar.
- Sometimes he compares hot girls by putting them below ugly ones.
- He spends years at zero and is so happy.

- He takes refuge in absurd activities to fill his life given his lack of success in the only thing that matters. So he studies, walks dogs, prepares classes, plays cards, watches soccer games, and other strange and inconsequential sports.

- He is interested in strange subjects in which he becomes a real walking encyclopedia.

- Minimizes your charisma, prestige, successes, and experience.

- Does not know who, how, where, or when to enter.

- Worries about unimportant things.

- Is unlikely to go out and about, let alone with you, and even less likely to go to the right places.

- Exalts other fools, or half-wits, putting them above you.

- He falls in love with the first one who appears and fails persistently in all his attempts of conquest.

- He does not shirk serious commitment to anyone and rushes to get married quickly and have children.

- SOME HAVE GIRLFRIENDS they don't like because they have something and because they don't think they can access anything better.

- Some kinder fools are surprised and hallucinated by the more discreet performances you do.

- If he goes out with you and sees you flirting he takes off and leaves you hanging.

- He's always tired and quietly goes about his business.

- He tells his love projects as great feats without having done anything yet and makes a fool of himself.

- Some are macho because they have doubts about their virility.

- He speaks ill of women.

- Lives on illusions, never on realities.

- He immediately seeks to bring out your defects to put you on his level.

- He is not competitive.
- Favors come.
- He is easily deluded.
- He tends to know a lot about computers.
- Usually likes chess, basketball and cycling.
- Many do not even finish high school with lousy jobs afterward.
- The vast majority are ugly, poorly dressed, or aged.
- They have no courage.
- If he has a girlfriend, he's a hunk and lives enslaved by her.
- He is sexually frustrated.
- He is content with his overweight physique.
- If he ever fucks, it is with fat, old, ugly, short, drunk, or a mixture of all of them.
- They have never engaged in anything sexually interesting.
- He is disgusted by the pussies he never sucks.
- He badmouths you to girls.
- You can't count on him for anything.
- His girlfriend is sexually unsatisfied and then we have to take care of her if she is hot which is very difficult.
- He likes to make it difficult for you to do live flirting action.
- He has no taste for risk, no taste for speed.
- He buys expensive, slow, and ugly cars.
- If the girlfriend leaves them they go into an infinite depression from which it will take them many years to get out, if they get out at all.
- They criticize successful people out of pure envy.
- Their presence goes unnoticed by beautiful girls.
- He tells everyone what he has done, no matter how ridiculous it is, and especially what he is going to do, which is never done.
- His girlfriends look at you with desire.
- He offers to take the girls home in the car at night, like a good free cab driver.
- He throws parties and doesn't invite you.

- He talks to friends' girlfriends and gets excited thinking he's flirting.

- Lives with their parents and never buys his apartment.

- Let himself be driven by his parents.

- Awful hairstyles.

- Talks excitedly about historical dates for him, such as anniversaries of engagements.

- He insists and insists after an aunt, year after year with no results.

- He tells his mother about his adventures.

- Virgins until 25 or more. Many 40. Some forever.

- They give them the thirty to zero in everything.

- Unpleasant voice.

- Has girlfriends and suffers from seeing them hook up with everyone but him.

- He falls in love with these girlfriends.

- Talks to girls for hours on end without carrying any danger.

- He plans and tells everyone what his love projects are going to be. Making an awful fool of himself, as they always fail.

- He brags about supposedly non-existent relationships. No matter how little interaction, he will already consider that he is with her. Or he considers that he has had a love relationship when he has met her twice without anything happening.

- His girlfriends cheat on them.

- He forms a gang with girls and spends the night talking to them without getting into any of them and those friends will never become anything more than friends.

- Sometimes it takes him great physical effort to go out at night and he is seen out there sweating and fatigued.

- His only opportunities in his head are girlfriends in the gang, which take long years to get. Those outside the gang are simply impossible.

- If you pick one up, he thinks she's your girlfriend.

- He frequents whorehouses.

- He likes to eat in the street, preferably eating disgusting things in front of girls.

- If he sees that some girl looks at you he hides it from you.

- The girls that he likes see him pissing in the middle of the street. Pure glamour.

- He exaggerates any small defect you may have to detract from your morale.

- He misses opportunities or doesn't look for them and between opportunity and opportunity, there is an abyss of time.

- His vacation time is not used to go to places where there is nothing to do, but to places where there is nothing to do.

- If there is a city with a lot to do, he will never go there.

- Some fools go out late and leave early, after visiting the least favorable places. Others go out at eight o'clock in the evening to drink seven calibers in a single sitting in a sleazy bar. These are the fewest. They leave the bar at eleven o'clock and at one o'clock they are at home drunk and vomiting, after having eaten a greasy hamburger, the only thing they got out of it.

clean.

- Others get drunk and go to sleep alone, without even talking to any of them. Spending a fortune for nothing.

- HE WILL ALWAYS BE able to criticize, to give himself airs of intellectual.

- Many, being grown up, have no apartment, no car, no job, no girlfriend, no friends, no beauty, no intelligence. Nothing.

- Saturday night always:

° They are sick.

° Very tired.

° They have work to do.

° They go out to the movies.

○ They go out to dinner.

○ They go out for a quiet evening.

- He eats in the street, preferably ice cream.

- He studies for competitive examinations many times without success and thus wastes long years of his life.

- He talks incessantly about his love projects, which never come to fruition in the end.

- He does not know or explore his environment.

- He wastes his weekend time on absurd trips and being with his family, which he does not leave until he is well past 40. Family, that is, his parents.

- Many fools have dogs because they keep them company.

- Few fools you will find with a pleasant voice.

- A good goatee is a complement that certifies that he is one.

- Silly phrases.

○ Here we are.

○ Let's see if anything falls.

○ I'm going hungry.

○ I'm going home.

○ I'm tired.

○ I have to prepare a paper.

○ I don't believe it.

○ We don't eat anything.

○ I get years with nothing.

○ I can't go out.

○ My friend.

○ I'm retiring early today.

○ I'm going quietly.

- The fool always talks about work and goes to places where nothing's cooking. He will always be seated and thinks he can afford to be quiet. He subtracts infinitely from you, contributes nothing, and on top of that he thinks he is smarter than you. He criticizes your successes and he marries the first fat woman (because they are always fat women) he picks up and is happy for life.

That's the life of a fool, my friends. A guy with no intelligence, no charisma, no experience, no beauty, no poise, no spark, who does everything wrong. A dull person who fails and who thinks he is better than you.

The Necktie Club.

This is a humorous fictional story that contains the essence of the values of the fool a little exaggerated, but it is really funny. Here it goes.

The Necktie Club

Purpose: To hold long get-togethers on Friday and Saturday nights to show that the night doesn't interest us, we're mature.

Entry requirements.

- Not to have had the slightest relationship with the opposite sex in the last five years. Not to have kissed a single person in that time.

- Dress in an old-fashioned way: bowler hat, umbrella, tie, trench coat, scarf, and shoes.

- Be over 30 years old, male, and single.

- Be a teacher, scholarship holder, researcher, or computer scientist.

- Go through life calmly, without haste. Because there is time!

- A lover of reading and coffee.

- Romantic and respectful with girls. They are pampered and showered with attention.

- Differentiate yourself from the young people being old and proud of it. Because we are not kids anymore, for God's sake!

- To have slow cars, that consume much and are expensive, to appear position.

- To like the Spanish music of the 80's. Mecano, Bose, Bebe and La Oreja.

- Looking for a serious, formal, and lasting relationship.

- Like long discussions of current affairs, globalization, climate change, or anything soporific.

- To like girls from good families, wealthy and of noble ancestry.

- To renounce to any modernity. For us always the classic.

- Conscious of equality, feminism, and the empowerment of women.

- Detest in action and intrigue movies. Drama and conventional humor. Movie buffs.

We vindicate the traditional man, good husband, good father, calm, patient conversationalist, traditional values, education, sobriety, culture, romanticism, and seriousness in the face of youthful madness.

How to impress the girls, according to the Necktie club.

Let them see that you spend money, they like that. You have to invite them.

- Have expensive things to show off, watches, brand name sweaters, colognes. Let them see you are posh.

- Give them gifts and details, like calling them on special dates.

- It is necessary to put in hours. The flirting is a thing of going little by little giving them confidence, the more you put in, the better.

- To have expensive cars that consume much, so that the economic power is seen.

- Call them as "you". That shows respect and distance.

- Go to the most expensive and traditional pubs. Where well-to-do people hang out. Preferably law students, economists, doctors, lawyers, notaries, and businessmen.

- Go for dinner before going out, that makes you fatter and therefore more mature, serious, and stable, which is what they like. Incidentally, it shows that there is an economic level.

- Persist and persist year after year even married to another, you never know.

- Accompany them home by car as a serious chauffeur, showing that you do not drink and you are prudent and reliable. More points in your favor.

- Give them roses, it makes an impact.

- TAKE TRIPS ABROAD, it shows economic power and culture.

    - To go to places of armchair and table, instead of places of march. That tells them you are serious.

    - Having a good belly, gives prestige, prestige and status.

    - Dress classic and brand name.

    - Insist over and over again. It will fall!

The essence of the fool.

When everything seemed to be known about the fool, one day at a meal I was horrified and suddenly I grasped the whole essence of the fool and it gave me a terrible shock. Maybe it was the wine, but the fact is that I tuned in and understood what were the guidelines of his behavior that are like poison that kills intelligence. I felt its horrible essence, which contaminates and destroys everything it touches. I tuned in to their mental attunement. This, my friends, is what I grasped as a possessed person, simply by looking at that character, who concentrated with absolute perfection, all the existing nonsense in his sad person.

This is what that wretch was thinking.

You have to give the image of a formal boy.

You have to be polite and gentlemanly.

It's good to ridicule yourself to make the girls laugh.

The beautiful thing is love.

There can be no sex without love and those who do it without love are crazy.

Girls have to take a lot of effort and it's better to never come out for fear of rejection than to try something.

Confident girls are scary.

You have to pay a lot of attention and go out of your way for the one you like.

At night there are only crazy girls who are not worth it.

All those who say they are flirting are ghosts and bad people.

I have to please girls to make them like me.

The precarious and poorly paid job leaves me with no strength to go out or meet people.

The proposals that are made to me are rejected for not being sufficiently formal.

As I am very responsible and work hard, I don't look for better things because there are none.

For a girl, I would do anything and I would give up everything for her. Girls should always be with me. Because I give them security and protection as well as fidelity.

Because I give them security and protection as well as one hundred percent fidelity.

I am a good guy who wants a single serious and lasting relationship for life.

The commitment, the children, and their cost, I will realize with hard work, even despite my health.

Beauty is fleeting and the sooner the little I have passed, the better. Because I want girls to appreciate my inner self, the confidence I give, and the responsibility I offer.

That beloved of mine would more than fulfill all my expectations.

Probably, I will never find another one as perfect as her.

It is better to fall in love and not be reciprocated than to go around trying to flirt.

If one day I were to pick up a girl, I would become her happy slave, without caring about anything else.

Parties and entertainment are for degenerates. I will meet the woman of my life by working, as it should be.

Prudence and respect for the rules must be taken to rajat-abla.

Better not to risk.

How does a guy become a
subject into a fool?

By failing in his efforts and being frustrated countless times, the subject develops a self-defense mechanism to save his impoverished self-esteem. So he sets up a world in which it is impossible to flirt and his reality is like that and consoles himself with this defeatist thought. He believes that he is normal and the world is full of people like him. In that world he is happy.

If someone breaks this illusion, the fool realizes that he is a poor wretch. Therefore, he hates the smart guy who humiliates him. Once this clever person disappears, the fool is once again convinced that this was not possible or was not compensated. He thinks a lot about the lack of compensation for what he was doing. And he feels good again, in his imaginary world that he will never leave. Envy and suspicion will be the only thing these characters will give you, as well as the most cruel and undeserved criticism.

One turn of the screw and the fool ends up in the psychiatric ward.

That's right friends, when a fool stays next to a winner, no matter how unnatural this situation may be, a spiral of miseries takes place, leading the poor fool not only to his previous level but to total tragedy.

but total tragedy. Despite the kindness of this winner who wants to help him, the fool does not assimilate the teaching and returns to his natural state. This fool has been stealing energies from the clever one, parasitizing, without contributing anything. On the contrary, he has harmed and damaged the strong. This phenomenon of nature is restored by the universe itself, and all that has been stolen from the fool remains at an unfathomable minimum. The smart recovers perfectly because he is strong. But this thief falls and falls until he crashes, never to get up again and the natural order is restored.

THE FOOL, EMBOLDENED by the teachings of the smart one, begins to believe that he can compete with him and that he no longer needs him. He doesn't realize that while the smart one succeeded with quality girls, he was with average ones or directly with awful girls. But from the quantity came the mistake. The domain, the seduction, the quality, of that, nothing at all, but how he was adding triumphs, he was trusting in him.

One day, emboldened, he enters the territory of the strong, where his abilities do not allow him to survive. The fort successfully defends its territory and he is massacred when he tries to compete for chicks that are not within his reach.

THE FOOL FELL IN LOVE and was harassed and beaten both by them and by the smart one. There begins his misfortune, his decline because instead of assimilating his defeat, he starts to get angry and becomes aggressive, unpleasant, threatening, and very very frustrated.

As he can't do anything with girls of that level, his madness and frustration are so high that he attacks the hand that feeds him, his smart friend. Jealousy, envy, and all his inferiority come to the surface. He tries to compete again and is overwhelmed. The clever one gets tired and decides to punish the fool. The fool receives a very hard and implacable punishment until his complete execution, having to see the triumphs of the clever one. Executed, beaten, and unanswered, the fool falls and falls into depression and madness and begins to lose the little knowledge he assimilated. He is no longer able to put them into practice. He will try to run away to save his self-esteem, he will hesitate, he will return, and each time he will receive one crushing after another. In this way, he becomes unbalanced and crazy. Until one day he does something crazy and is committed to the psychiatric hospital, where sordid characters make him even crazier.

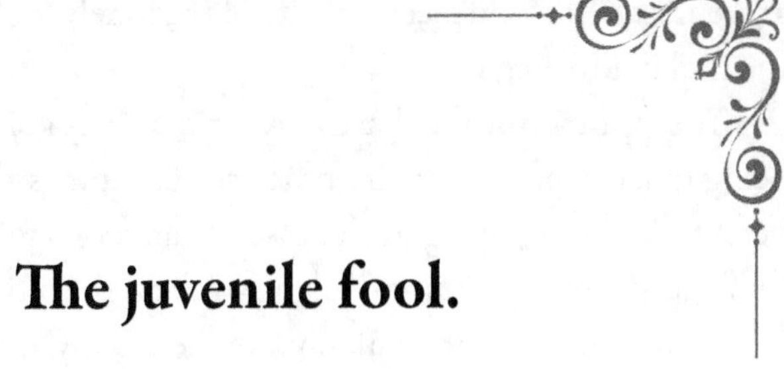

The juvenile fool.

The fool lives immersed in his alienation, living under shackles that he has put on himself because of his lack of determination and resolution that minimizes his already minimal attractiveness.

The fool is often given to eating and is prone to put on weight. His clothes go unnoticed as well as his person and even more his personality. The fool past the age of 21 goes even less, because, at that point, he has already lost all hope and gives up. At this point, it is better to take pity on him.

The fools get together and so the fears and fears of each one are passed on to the others and they all become dumber, believing that this is normal. The fool lives in the world of fools and is completely alien to the normal world. In the world of fools, the most fun one can have is to talk with fools about foolish things, to eat cakes and pastries that make you fat. In the world of fools, all the girls who live there are ugly and dull. They are the fools, and they are the only women available to him in this world.

The answer of these women to the amorous proposals of the fool is always No! And the few times that they say yes, it is to say again, No! soon after. In the world of the fools, to get a girl is the labor of many, many years, almost always lustrums.

The natural state of the fool is the eternal infatuation and in the fantasy of the fool, there are loved ones, but not lovers, who will never answer him. The fool persists and persists without the least pride. Again and again, he crashes into failure, until one day, by chance, he triumphs and ends the fool's life, and the life of the lonely fool ends, and the life of the fool in love begins.

The fool and the fool have a great time never going out, studying, and being quiet. Fun and sex are otherworldly things they have never tried before. Without paying in the case of the fool and they couldn't fit the fool's head. Eating cakes and taking a walk is the ultimate action for these fools. The fools do not drink nor are they funny, nor do they know how to talk about anything, they only know how to keep quiet and at most criticize. Monotony is the tonic and so on forever.

The fool usually falls in love, but some fools are not satisfied with that, they also fail in their studies and they are very abundant. Normally, the fool does not eat a donut and on top of that, repeats the course. He will be unsuccessful in his binge drinking, he will plan his exams poorly and he will see everything in a rosy light. At the end of the course, he will find himself the same as he was, a year older, in the same course, and with the same black prospects.

He does not devote himself to women because he is not very intelligent. For this, is the most interesting thing to do. If he is not dedicated to it, it is quite logical that he does not know how to apply his brain to studies either. Unless he puts a lot of effort into hours and hours of study, which a normal person does in a tenth of the time, he will not pass. That is why it is normal that the fool either fails and passes with flying colors, or fails.

HE DOESN'T REALIZE that while the smart one succeeded with quality girls, he was with average ones or directly with awful girls. But from the quantity came the mistake. The domain, the seduction, the quality, of that, nothing at all, but how he was adding triumphs, he was trusting in him.

One day, emboldened, he enters the territory of the strong, where his abilities do not allow him to survive. The fort successfully defends its territory and he is massacred when he tries to compete for chicks that are not within his reach.

The fool fell in love and was harassed and beaten both by them and by the smart one. There begins his misfortune, his decline because instead of assimilating his defeat, he starts to get angry and becomes aggressive, unpleasant, threatening, and very very frustrated.

As he can't do anything with girls of that level, his madness and frustration are so high that he attacks the hand that feeds him, his smart friend. Jealousy, envy, and all his inferiority come to the surface. He tries to compete again and is overwhelmed. The clever one gets tired and decides to punish the fool. The fool receives a very hard and implacable punishment until his complete execution, having to see the triumphs of the clever one. Executed, beaten, and unanswered, the fool falls and falls into depression and madness and begins to lose the little knowledge he assimilated. He is no longer able to put them into practice. He will try to run away to save his self-esteem, he will hesitate, he will return, and each time he will receive one crushing after another. In this way, he becomes unbalanced and crazy. Until one day he does something crazy and is committed to the psychiatric hospital, where sordid characters make him even crazier.

The fool´s girl.

The fool is a bland, ugly, bitter, or stupid woman. Her failure is so great that non-fools run away from her. This bimbo will spoil the party for all her friends. She'll be the first to go home, she'll be the first to go home, she'll be the first to go home.

the first to go home, she will be the tired, the bland, and the dull one. Depression is her natural state, which she fosters by making a fuss over every guy who approaches her, to do her a real favor. And on top of that, she will reject it, continuing her life in depression.

Sometimes she cries for no reason and feels like a victim. She tries to attract attention and criticize the lively, cheerful, and animated women, whom she will label as irresponsible madwomen. Her next state will be the spinster and her life a real failure.

Entrance to the pub of a fool.

The fool enters with his head down, with a tired, bored, and unsure step. In good faith, no girl has noticed that this has happened. The fool doesn't know any of them, something that doesn't seem to worry this to worry this unhappy man. He doesn't smile, doesn't talk to anyone, doesn't look at the girls and they are indifferent to his person and his personality. The first thing he will have thought of is to go to the bar, to have a couple of betas, to have strength, or maybe a pineapple juice. He asks with

a) Shy voice.

Or

b) Ordinary voice.

His consumption.

Done this, the fool will form with his gregarious ones a well-closed circle. Composed of ugly, fools and friends, if any. The chosen place will be as far away as possible from the march. There, between comments about how tired they are, they will tell their jokes. They will encourage some stupid conversation, on any monotonous subject, absolutely absent from their surroundings. If the fool pretends to get out of this circle of horror, he will be harshly reproached by the other fools. A good average fool emboldened, will approach girls in this order:

First the lifelong girlfriends. To which he will fuck the night and they will not be able to flirt. Because neither flirts nor leaves. He will tell them with a tired, monotonous, and boring air.

MONOTONOUS AND BORING, totally inappropriate serious topics, without letting the others speak. In short, he will give them a hard time. The fool will harass them and will look at their cleavage, which will be what he will get out of the night and thus he will have his image for the straw. If the fool by any chance did not have traps to fall into and would have avoided:

(a) Tiredness.

b) The circle of fools.

c) The friends.

He would arrive at the right point by pure chance. But here he will demonstrate with an unspeakable forcefulness, his absolute nullity for women. And very soon he will return, to his circle of fools, from where he should have left, never!

The market rejects the fool's insinuations and puts everyone in their place. Some of them fucking beautiful women and others talking about turbot with cockatoos. Thus the market, which is fair but cruel to the weak, will put the fool in his place. To kill himself with handjobs. It will not allow the clever to go hungry.

The fool's incursion will be at random, without having looked at anything. He will enter boringly to some strangers. Normally he will push the pretty ones aside to enter the ugly ones and if he does not do it, the pretty ones will immediately ignore him and he will get a little more depressed. The fool will immediately lend himself to buying drinks, to see if something falls out. His sophomoric role will not be able to be endured for long. The look stuck in the bra, a ridiculous little dance and you can already hear the comments and distress signals emitted by the girls. But it's when he's harassing you and comes closer and closer, giving his never-ending lecture, that the poor girls can't take it anymore, and they invent anything to get out of there, suffocated and terrified. The fool will come back to you later and tell you that he has done a great performance, or better yet, that they are in the boat. After a while, he will go home to dream his illusions, which will never be fulfilled. And he will think, he has very little left to be a great flirt.

Types of attack of the fool.

Attack type A. Drunk lost.

The fool will be drunk and lost, talking loudly, with his eyes almost blank, his shirt splattered with liquor, sweaty and aggressive. Stiff from bending over to talk to dwarves. Vociferating at old, fat, ugly, short, short, and pale. Who are the only ones he considers himself capable of flirting with? The fool will always carry a good so-bre peso, five drinks too many, and a pretentious jacket, full of lampoons. If he can limp, so much the better. This attack makes them flee in a very wide radius and everyone who sees him escapes. The clothes are horrible, wrinkled, and at least fifteen years old. He is unshowered and smells bad.

Attack type B. Stalker

Staring at the tits, harassing and standing in front of them for a long time even if they don't look at him or talk to him. He is still standing there. He will make little shouts to get their attention like a bullfighter and will continue his soporific role. When by chance one looks at him out of compassion, the mechanism is activated and he continues to be a pain in the ass. His head wobbles and he stalks hesitantly. He also pays for drinks and buys roses.

Entrance to the same pub of a smart guy.

He enters with confidence, smiling, and has gait, strength, and charisma.

He glances inside smiling at the doorman and immediately sees interesting girls. Maybe the ones he met the other day or some old fans. He talks to them in a friendly way, but without wasting time, and goes with a confident step to the dance floor, or the area with the most going on, keeping a watchful eye on the girls. As soon as he arrives, he notices their agitation. Some of them whisper, others look furtively. Others stare until they realize he sees them. The waitresses smile at him when he orders something. He feels triumphant and they sense it right away. There are many of his innumerable exes swarming around. He ignores them and when he studies the terrain, he attacks with devastating conviction, elegance, and good work. The girls appreciate him, some even introduce themselves to him, there are murmurs and nudges as he passes by. Some of them even drop their drinks when they see him. In short, he can choose, he knows it and he does it. He works infinitely good girls, that the fool in his miserable life will taste. He smiles a winning smile and succeeds with ease and ease. He is serene calm and confident and usually leaves the pub with:

A known hottie.

With a phone number, he's got.

With a new girl, he has met there who is very horny.

With a girl, he has hooked up with there.

In the end, he gets clean phone numbers, hot girls, great times, and more confidence and prestige.

A little class for Jesus Christ!

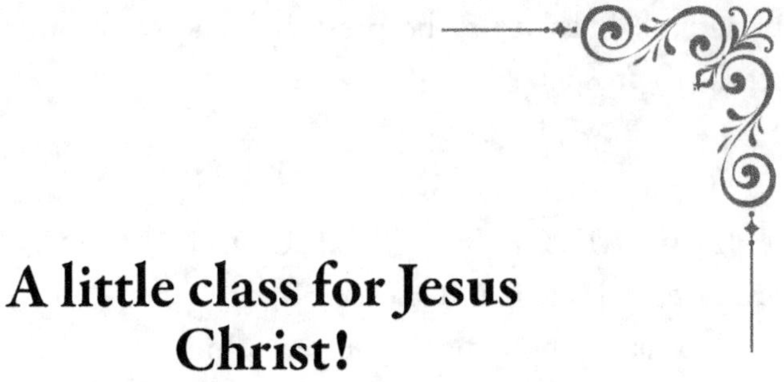

-I was a little burnt out on this narrative of lazy guys who never moved forward. You have to help but also stay away from toxic people like

but also stay away from toxic people like these".

Do not accept the company of mediocre men, even if they claim to be great admirers and flatterers of yours. No matter how many compliments and acknowledgments they give, what do they contribute? Less than nothing.

Under the trick of their submission, they hide a whole arsenal of apoc-amino, bravado, fantoche, and lousy self-esteem. That no matter how much they want to hide and give their best version, it exists and diminishes.

People get together with those who have the same self-esteem. The union of one with another of lower self-esteem can only have one result: catastrophe! Fears, insecurities, embarrassments, mediocre lives. They instill their world and their problems and even if you think you are safe, they will affect you.

You can't be the good Samaritan who helps for nothing.

If you give to a fool, don't expect to get anything in return, or think you are doing a good deed. Everyone has to be in their place. Winners and losers.

Nature is wise and has no mercy. That quality of api-adding to the fool and trying to lift him to where he should never have been is unnatural. It is not to be produced, the weak must succumb for the strong to prosper.

THE WEAK HAVE LOW QUALITY, low dominance, and low leverage, and that is as it should be.

No matter how much you teach him, time and time again he will come back! To his average level, where he is comfortable, in mediocrity.

Never let it be said to me! That encouragement should be given to the weak, the foolish, or the coward. For they are subjects who deserve to be where they are. On the contrary, humiliate them if they accidentally come into contact with you. Total contempt.

As I once said. What I recognize is this, NOTHING! And I insist once again on not only not helping but sinking and annihilating your horrible presence once and for all. And may you never be associated with anyone of that ilk.

I don't care if he is a fool or a foolish fool. I am ashamed, I am discredited by his mere presence near me. There is nothing to be proud of them and they certainly don't represent me. A disgrace.

Gentuza!

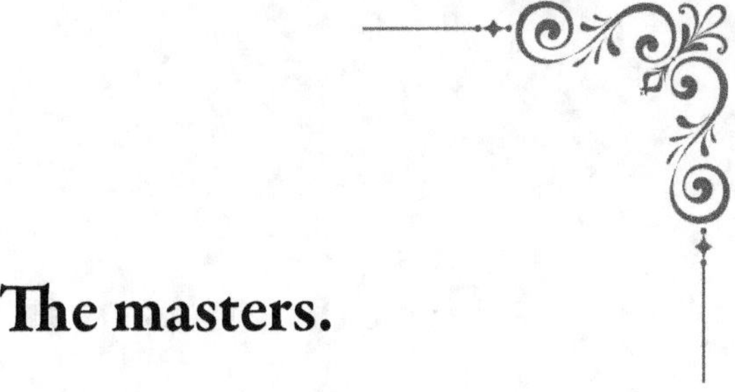

The masters.

There is a type of fool who is the so-called scholar. This fool takes refuge in the studies given the scarce possibilities that he has with the girls. So he will study a career, do a thesis, a dissertation, a doctorate, or a postgraduate course, and do everything he can to extend his career.

everything he can to extend his studies.

But it is in the masters where he feels at ease and so he will dedicate himself to studying master's degree after master's degree. If possible, of exaggeratedly long duration. He fills his years with this occupation.

He will be able to say that he is a very cultivated man or a man with a lot of studies and he will hide behind this. This man's companions are like him. When he sees them, he says they are phenomena, cracks. I say that for me they are fools. The more they study, the worse it is. What have these people done?

And so they give him 50 years with a ridiculous experience and probably a virgin. That's what masters are for, to fill that time. This fool doesn't try anything with the girls, he already has the mas-te

rs and there he is until retirement doing masters.

The demands of the fool.

To justify his lack of creation in the field of love, the fool will make very high demands. Thus, for a fool already well into his forties, only girls of a maximum of 33 years old, without children of 1.70 to above, very beautiful, nice, charming, with higher studies and the most important thing, of a good family, will be satisfactory.

most importantly, from a good family.

Thus, his impoverished self-esteem can say that he doesn't go with any of them because only those are of the level he requires. So, either he goes with those, or he doesn't go with any of them. On top of that, he thinks he belongs to the elite. The reality is that he has never been with girls like that, he has been a virgin for at least 15 years, and he will continue to be so.

The thesis.

Another good pastime of the fool is to do theses and dissertations that will take years. The chosen topics will be the most s-

The chosen topics will be the most outlandish that you can imagine, so these will be done on:

The Pyrenean Great Bustard.

Turbot breeding.

The economic exploitation of salmon trout.

The economic crisis in the 16th century.

The influence of feudalism in contemporary society.

The reproduction of the Hispanic pike.

The wine exploitation in eastern Lapland.

The Australian penguin.

The short-snouted red kangaroo.

The Serengeti monkey.

All of them, of burning actuality. To which he dedicates many years of research and in the interactions with the girls these topics are brought up as an interesting colloquium.

The professors of these theses are usually nerds, much younger than him, with zero or tending to zero experience, and on top of that, they send him.

Time management.

There is always time to start to overwhelm, to begin to ar-radar in the market. You have more than enough knowledge to be a reference in the field of seduction. What happens is that they are very busy studying their thesis, master's, and other studies. So with one or two outings a year, they have more than enough to shake the market with their performances. And of course, they will find the girl they are looking for, about 30 years old or younger, pretty, and from a good family.

less, pretty, and from a good family.

But for now, they are very busy studying all this. They have a lot of responsibilities, work, studies, and obligations and they can't devote themselves to getting an aunt, understandably. That's why until they are sixty there is time, there is no hurry, calmly, things slowly and well.

The cartwheels and sangria.

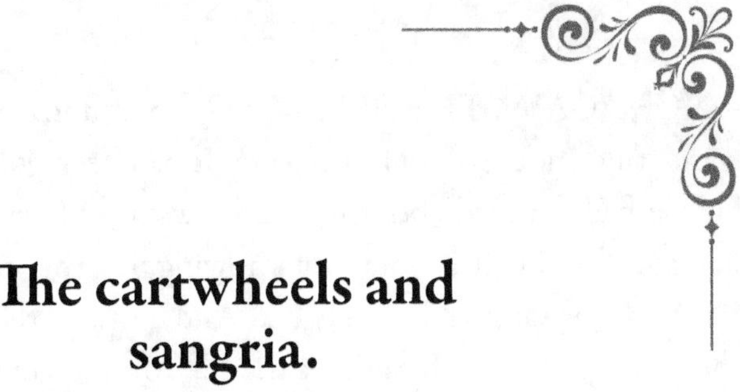

Once at a beach party back in the 90s, all the fools came. It was a party, but the fools were engaged in a sort of contest to see who could do the biggest somersault. Instead of doing the right things and talking to the girls, they started to do drunken cartwheels. What I am telling you is true. That's how it was. One did a good cartwheel, then it was another one, who did a bigger one.

The girls hallucinated watching these guys, already 20 years old and were at the mercy of the smart ones.

In a moment of frenzy, one of the fools stuck his head in a vat full of sangria and pulled his head out dripping hair and face with sangria.

Another fool's retort was to lose his keys and money in one of the somersaults.

He said, "Holy shit! I had lost the keys and the money- And there we were for a long time looking for it, but it did not appear.

At that time the fools wandered along the promenade, going up to any girl who appeared and saying: "Hello, what's your name" and after a while, they would say: "Shall we make out?

They always said no. Then the fool went to consult you why he did not flirt and said. -I enter them, I tell them, I see that you can't handle the liter. Let me help you. What fails me is the second step. They came in by the hundreds, and they did not flirt at all, but at least they tried. Not like others who chicken out. There are many kinds of fools. These were fun fools. They had a lot of nerve.

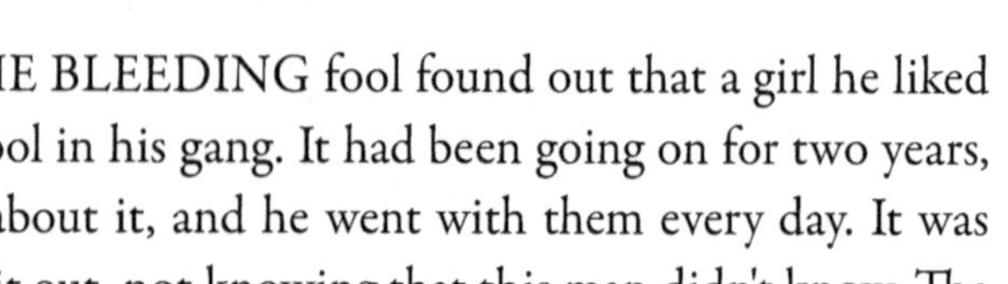

ONCE AGAIN, THE BLEEDING fool found out that a girl he liked was dating another fool in his gang. It had been going on for two years, but he hadn't heard about it, and he went with them every day. It was my fault for blurting it out, not knowing that this man didn't know. The fool with the sangria drew a blank. And he asked the other fool who was there, that is, the boyfriend, his friend, "Are you going out with her? The other one said, "Yes, for two years already.

That same night he went out, in this case with a five-liter can of sangria and drank all five liters. He had to be carried home dragging his feet across the floor, mangled and fatal. An eyewitness reported that the fool was lifting a can, making a physical effort that could injure his back because of the weight he was lifting. He said, "He was giving himself a "kidney" of blood-letting".

How could it be that the poor fool never came back to this place and we didn't know more about him until 20 years later, when he was already married? The worst moment of his life, poor man. What did I know?

That same girl of the sangria fool, they all liked her and the other two fools in the gang were also in love. The three of them formed a fantastic triumvirate. This girl from the gang was all these men aspired to. All three of them managed to date her. Bravo for them. But in the end, none of them did. And you can see how one of them turned out. The girl was average to ugly.

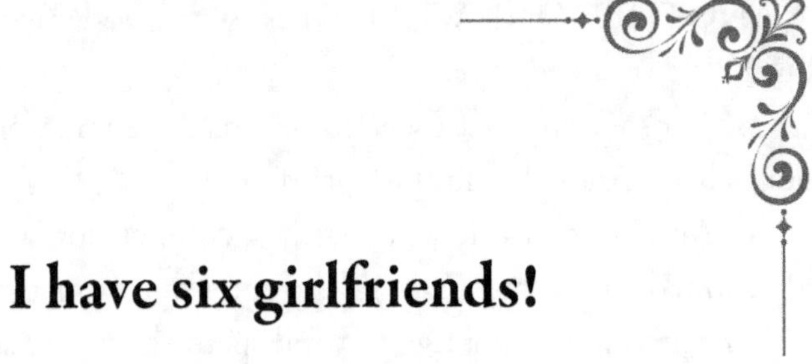

I have six girlfriends!

There were three very prominent fools. I'll call them the sangria fool, the pineapple juice fool, and the motorcycle fool.

Let's talk about the pineapple juice fool who made some brutal performances in those years.

The first days of summer we would get together all the local guys and talk about the new girls that had appeared in the apartments. Someone was in charge of talking to them and bringing them to the group of friends to meet them, then we used to organize a party on the beach.

They were cute cute girls from 18 to 21 years old and we were 22 or 23 years old. All of them were beautiful interesting attractive girls with good bodies, each one tried to give a good image, and the silly pineapple juice amazed all and sundry with legendary performance.

The first day was so to speak the official introduction of the new girls to the group of friends. When they were all with us, this man did this.

The girls asked him, "And are you with any girls? The pineapple juice fool answered instantly.

-I have six girlfriends!

1. one from my school who is a brunette and has fat tits.

2. Another one who is short but has an ass!

3. Another one who's at the gym where I go who smiles at me and talks to me sometimes.

4. ANOTHER ONE WHO comes to the academy with me, she's hot but I haven't talked to her.

5. Another one that I see on the street, well that one has a boyfriend but I also consider her my girlfriend.

6. And another one who was in a competition and left the door of her room open for me. I was able to enter but, I am a gentleman-.

The girls were flabbergasted and spent the whole summer using him to drive them to and from pubs, like a free cab driver. The good friend, the teddy bear.

The pineapple juice fool at the beach parties used to drink three liters of pineapple juice while telling dirty jokes. He would say, "I'm a sportsman, I don't drink alcohol," and he would tell jokes and bad jokes that would scare the girls.

Another day he said, "The day I pick up a girl, I'm going to take her to the apartment and I'm not going to come back all night. He said that in 1994 and we had to wait until 2003 for him to pick up. Because he gave her the whole decade of the come to zero and the first one who flirted with her married her and it was a disaster of a marriage.

At another party, he started beating his chest and saying "I'll be back". Because he thought he was a Terminator. In a game, he had to make out with the girl that all these guys liked and he kissed her on the bo-ca, he went home all happy. He told his mother- I went with Juanin and we played kissing games with the girls and I kissed xxxx-.

Another day he said to some girls - Here on this bench I gave my first kiss, my first kiss was when I was 20 years old - And he was already 25 or so.

Another day he grabbed a girl by the back in the pool and said -We are mated- The girls ran away.

At that kissing party as he called it. He asked one who we called "the board" because she was so flat, "Why are you wearing a bra if you don't have any?

My grandmother said, "That boy is subnormal, he looks like a monkey. What a gum! He has never flirted in his life, nor is he going to flirt, because he's stupid -and we didn't tell her anything about these performances, she could already tell just by looking at him.

ON ANOTHER OCCASION, my mother and my aunt were sitting on a bench and he goes and sits there with them and said to them- such a girl has come, I like that girl, I like her, I like her,- and he begins to tell them that he wanted to go out with her, that he thought she was very interesting, that he liked her very much. And that he wanted to give her a shake. The women convinced him not to do anything and he told them his plans. They were dying of laughter and could hardly contain their laughter at the sight of him.

Another day, also in front of the parents and friends of the parents, he blurts out, "I have to find a girl now, even if it's a chubby one!

Another time my mother was there and my mother said to him, "Juanin has been in France, he has seen the French girl, he was with her there". And he thought to ask, "Did he do her?

This "did he do her" is the expression they use in this place to refer to "did he fuck her" but of course my mother didn't know anything about that and thought: "Did he do her? What did he do to her? And she thought it was a handjob and said: "I don't know anything about those things". She came back freaked out at how dumb it was. Even the Mothers were freaking out.

Another time, there was one who liked him and had touted to everyone that he was going to ask her out to dinner and then ask her if she wanted to go out with him. The specific line was. "You'll see, I'm attracted to you, we could go out if you want and if it doesn't go well then we'll stop and that's it" What do you say, huh? What do you say? He had it all rehearsed and everything and he just blurted it out without looking at her.

Twenty minutes after finishing dinner, he was back home having failed. There were even bets on what was going to happen. Nobody bet on him. More like betting on how long the dinner would last.

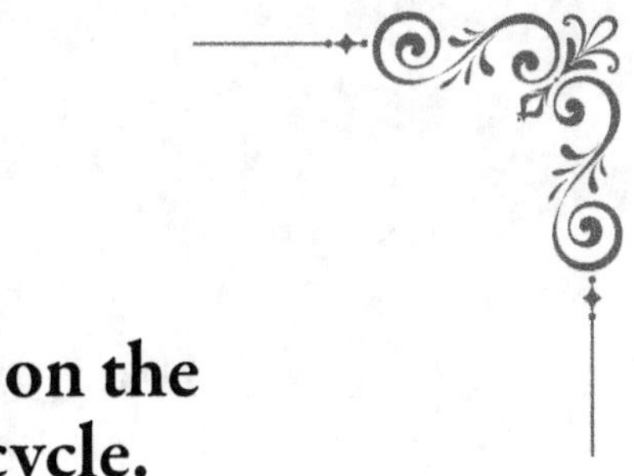

The fool on the motorcycle.

This is the one who dated the longest with this girl that all three of them liked. He had a motorcycle and one day he was outside the pub riding his motorcycle crazy and he got hit by his trunk in full view of the whole pub and was left with a bloody face. He went to get patched up and turned up with stitches and band-aids.

and showed up with stitches and band-aids all over his face.

Back in the pub, he asked a woman if she wanted to go for a ride with him on the motorcycle.

Another day, he went to the beach party and started to tease the French girl, asking her, "Are you from France? So, you must speak French. Here we speak Spanish. How do you say rum? You say gon and it's rum.

Then she threw a live crab at one of them and it slipped into her tits. Finally, the girls got up, pushed him, and kicked him out of the party insulting him. They told him -Get out of here you idiot- and he left saying -They are in love with me-.

The gynephobe.

I racked my brain a lot, trying to understand, why a foolish acquaintance of mine never went with girls. That if he's gay, that if the family imposes too high standards, that if he's a workaholic,

that he's not hormonal and is asexual. I no longer knew what explanation to find for his lack of effort in this regard. I would pass him a blank decade and he would be so calm. I was already having a hard time seeing him, because of the strange things I thought about him. However, one day I discovered what was wrong with him.

What was wrong with him was simply that he was afraid of girls, so I looked on the internet and there I found it, gynephobia.

Instead of partying at the medieval fair where we were all friends, he was in a lab with a geek. Doing strange statistical studies. In the middle of July with all the heat, on a Sunday!

That's why this man does everything necessary to avoid contact with women. Now things are explained. That's where the masters come from, that's where it all comes from.

He is terrified. If someone gives him the phone he doesn't call her, that's why he sets such high standards that are impossible to meet, to justify the fact that he does nothing. Virgin, virgin with almost 50 years, and this in 2019 will continue to add years to zero. Calculate yourselves because he is not going to flirt anymore.

He once got a girl totally into him for the money. Because this man has. He wasn't doing anything and she had to be the one

WHO SAID, "I LIKE YOU," and then he went in and kissed her. That day he didn't do anything else and they made a date for another day. She said, "You invite me to dinner and I'll invite you to breakfast," and so he invited her to dinner and then he went home to his house where he lives with his parents at 47 years old and the next morning he called her to go to breakfast.

Another girl wanted to sleep with him. I told him so and showed him the messages she was sending me about him. He politely declined the offer.

We were very indignant about the whole thing. If he were gay, I think it's fine, I prefer that he gets rid of it once and for all, what I don't like is that he pretends to be selling something he is not. He has a whole life with a very serious problem in this field.

More foolish actions.

I gather a group of girls at a party in an apartment and I am talking to them about an economic issue, which neither suits them nor suits them and rather bothers them.

rather annoys them. That's when I get my mouth out and I make a good party.

In the summer months, I isolate myself in a lab to continue doing strange studies with virgin freaky wankers.

I do a three-year master's degree, during which, despite having said I was going to go out and make an effort to look for girls, I don't go out during those years. Practically one day a year I go out on my own, of course. All this, without having any need to do so and without it being of any use to me. Only to continue doing strange studies. In an infinite loop that started at the end of the nineties and still does not end.

A lot of work, a lot of responsibilities, a lot of sacrifice, a lot of stress, I have no time for anything. And a friend goes and answers him: "The only responsibility you have is to take a hot girl and fuck her! That's your responsibility! Take responsibility for that!

Correcting exams, marking grades, attending meetings, teacher meetings, parent-teacher meetings, talking to parents, teaching. Meanwhile, others are on the beach with a hot chick with absolutely no worries whatsoever.

Saturday night I make myself a hot tea and go to bed to rest.

IN ONE OF THESE SEASONS, the hare may jump, take the cat out of the water, the flute may sound, and win a championship. The future is yet to be written. -But how is he going to do it, if he never goes out and never gets into social networks? Look at his language, one of these seasons, not one of these days. The triumphs that will come will be by luck, not by his own merits, according to his own words. Where are we going with this mentality?

In summer I don't take vacations and I keep on working. Although I am the boss of the company and I could delegate to someone else, I take responsibility and continue working.

The cockroach.

There was a guy in the late 90s, specifically in '99, that I met in Pontevedra.

A handsome guy of 1.95 m, well-dressed, well-dressed, with a good family. Well, this man was dumped by his girlfriend and was not in depression, but the following. At first, I didn't believe what he was saying and thought he was pulling my leg.

-We don't eat anything," he said without anyone asking him anything, and I thought, what a horny guy, this guy must be a great flirt!

But no, he wasn't flirting. What he did was get drunk at an exaggerated level. He would drink up to 20 birrillas he said, that is, one-third of a liter tubes, at a supersonic speed compulsively before starting to go to the interesting pubs.

At around one o'clock, he would start to get lazy, which is when the march began and he would soon be gone. I arrived at midnight in Pontevedra, which is 60 kilometers away, and at 1 o'clock I was already stranded. If I saw you talking to a girl, she would say, "You're losing your "cigarillo" and what about the school gas? - Protesting that he was not being listened to.

One night he and I went to Sanxenxo and there drinking his liters of beer he told me -I'm very hungry, I would fuck anything, even a cockroach would fuck me - that's how he got the nickname. That same night there were two girls in a pub and I saw them receptive. So I went, I met them and one of them, after 10 seconds of talking to me, leaned towards me, at à distance that I knew was not normal. So there in front of the cockroach,

I GAVE HER A SNOG AND the cockroach screamed - He's already eating her! Amazed and all fucked up.

The cockroach's fame grew and he became a sort of myth. A year later I got myself a very pretty girlfriend, azafa-ta, with green eyes, who was very hot and beautiful. I had told her about the cockroach and told her the funniest anecdotes. There we went to see what was in Pontevedra and to see if we could find the mythical cu-caracha and we did find him!

We entered the typical pub where the Cucaracha used to go and suddenly, we saw a mass above all the others, advancing wobbling. Yes, it was "the cockroach".

He sees me and says, "How handsome you are, you bastard, how well you live. And who is she? Your girlfriend? What a hot chick! How lucky you are, motherfucker. The girlfriend goes and says, "Hello, cockroach!

-Don't fucking call me that.

Real conversation that happened.

Girlfriend- Where did you come from?

Cockroach- I've just failed and at one o'clock I'm going to the envelope.

Girlfriend: Who did you fail with?

Roach- I think I just came from going into a pub waitress who is eighteen, she said no. (He was 30).

Girlfriend- But isn't she too young for you?

Cockroach: She's hot.

Girlfriend: So what are you going to do now?

Cockroach: I'm going to enter all the hens in the pub and at 1 o'clock I'm going to the envelope.

Girlfriend: And have you had a lot to drink? Cockroach: Ten birrillas and 6 Cubatas.

Then the cockroach started his round of the pub. He tapped them, they turned around, he saw them and said -bah- and he didn't get them in anymore. He asked one of them, "What's your name? and she answered "Deborah" and said, "I'm going to devour you".

I was so calm with my girlfriend and all of a sudden I noticed that they touched my ass from behind. There was the cockroach and he said to me, "Let me, man, I'm hungry!

The bride was amazed, but amazed at the loss. She said to me, "Reality surpasses fiction, you fell short".

Then we were laughing remembering the performances of the cu-caracha and she imitating him, invented one that gave us a fit of laughter. She said.

-At home, I have a wall with a hole in it, and I'm there, I'm trying to catch him until the wall falls ".

That was the cockroach, a guy whose greatest illusion was to fuck the hens (that's what he called the girls) and who almost ended up gay because of the hunger he went through.

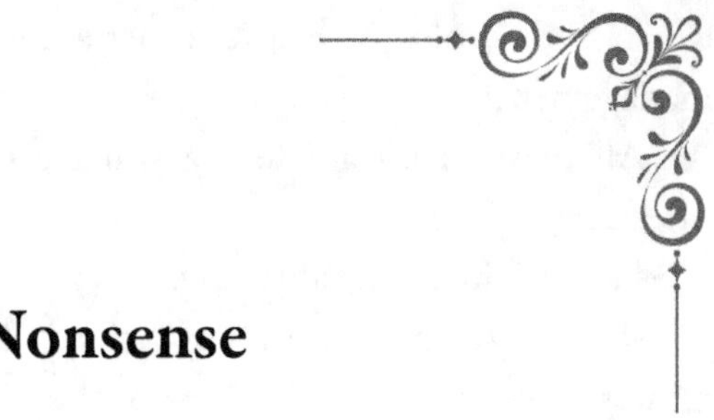

Nonsense

Saturday night, a hot tea, and off to bed.

49-year-old virgin and giving lessons to others.

People think he's gay and do nothing to disprove it.

If a girl calls and is interested, he gives her the runaround and never meets up with her.

I appreciate it but I'm too busy right now, he tells them.

Day of partying, wasted studying for some absurd master's degree.

Master's degree he doesn't need at all because they already have a very good job.

The fool could sell all his businesses and live on whatever they give him for the rest of his life just fine. But he prefers to be working sacrificing himself. He could also delegate and be rich enjoying his free time, because he could never work. But he works.

Neither in the back nor in the front. He doesn't get gay, doesn't pick up girls, he's stuck. Nobody understands him. Gynephobia.

Two little outings a year, both without doing anything, quietly, as if he were sober. And until next year.

Another decade at zero closes. There is time.

Loneliness, do you know what loneliness is? Loneliness is the gynephobic's dick.

A dick that no one sees, no one visits. It is in the deepest cell in an abandoned psychiatric hospital in the most depopulated lands of Soria. Locked and the key was thrown at the bottom of the black lagoon. What abandonment!

51 years old with the experience of a 15-year-old. What a management!

All these that I am telling you are real bleeding cases, I am not inventing anything.

I am not inventing anything.

"I like to play with my friend Manolito", that song is an understatement.

You invite me to dinner and I'll invite you to breakfast..." He invites her to dinner, and instead of going home and having sex, the gynophore goes to his parent's house the next morning he meets her and she invites him to breakfast. What would this woman think? Can you get any more ridiculous than that?

Let's play!

Don't miss out!

Visit the website below and you can sign up to receive emails whenever John Danen publishes a new book. There's no charge and no obligation.

https://books2read.com/r/B-A-FUKJ-TVVEC

BOOKS 2 READ

Connecting independent readers to independent writers.

Did you love *The Fool's Book*? Then you should read *How to Become a Real Man. Be an Alpha Male*[1] by John Danen!

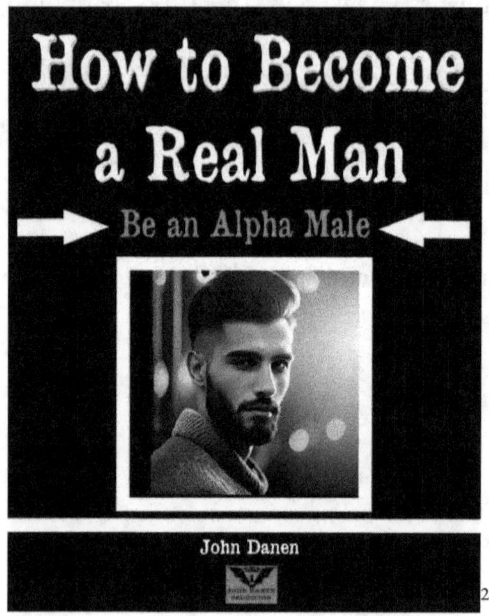

[2]

This book teaches you how to be a real man. Confident, determined and satisfied to be what he is.

A virile and strong man. A man who exudes masculinity. Because there is no better thing in life than being a man.

1. https://books2read.com/u/4AjZkk

2. https://books2read.com/u/4AjZkk

Also by John Danen

Seduction 5.0

S.A.X.

Chicas complicadas

Seducción 5.0

El libro del tonto

Macho Alpha

Macho alpha extracto

La seducción después de la pandemia

Terriblemente atractivo

Seducción 5.1

Sedução 5.1

How to be Cool and Attractive

Sedução. Avançada. X.

Garotas complicadas

¡Basta de ser buen chico! Sé un chico malo.

El método JD. El método de seducción de John Danen

El arte de agradarte a ti mismo

¡Basta ya de abusos! ¡Defiéndete!

Enought with the abuse! Defend yourself!

Máster en seducción

Las mujeres. El amor. Y el sexo.

Supera la dependencia emocional

Atrae mujeres con masculinidad

JD Absoluta seducción

El fracaso del amor

Entender a las mujeres
La vida del seductor sinvergüenza y encantador.
El arte de la dureza
Terrivelmente atraente
Deixe de ser um bom da fita! Seja um mauzão.
Superar a dependência emocional
A arte de se agradar
Pare o abuso! Defenda-se!
O fracasso do amor.
O método JD
Don´t Be a Good Boy! Be a Badass
Overcome Emotional Dependency
Complicated girls
The Art of Pleasing Yourself
Duro y Sinvergüenza
Mestre en sedução
JD Method
The Failure of Love. The Trap of Serious Relationships
Master in Seduction
A. S. X. Advanced. Seduction. X
Women. Love. Sex
How to Become a Real Man. Be an Alpha Male
Attract Women with Masculinity
JD Absolut Seductión
Understanding Women
The Life of the Shameless and Charming Seducer.
The Art of Toughness
Tough and Shameless
Überwindung der Emotionalen Abhängigkeit
Maître en séduction
Schrecklich Attraktiv
Surmonter la Dépendance Émotionnelle
L'art de la dureté

Die Kunst der Zähigkeit
Hör auf, ein guter Junge zu sein, sei ein böser Junge
Assez D'être un Bon Garçon ! Sois un Mauvais Garçon.
Die Kunst, sich Selbst zu Gefallen
Dur et sans Vergogne
Hart im Nehmen und Schamlos
L'art de se Plaire à soi-Même
Das Scheitern der Liebe
L'échec de L'amour.
Meister der Verführung
Die JD-Methode
Maestro di Seduzione
Terriblement Attrayant
La Méthode JD
Capire le donne
Compreendendo as Mulheres
Comprendre les Femmes
Die Frauen Verstehen
Les Filles Compliquées
Komplizierte Mädchen
JD Séduction Absolue
La Vie du Séducteur Charmant et sans Vergogne
Les Femmes. L'amour. Et le Sexe.
Mâle Alpha
S.A.X.
V.F.X.
Donne. Amore. E il sesso.
Ragazze Complicate
Superare la Dipendenza Emotiva
Seduzione. Avanzata. X.
Dark Seducción
Il Fallimento Dell'amore.
Il Metodo JD

Alphamännchen
Atrair Mulheres com Masculinidade
Attirare le donne con la Mascolinità
Attirer les Femmes par la Masculinité
Mit Männlichkeit Frauen Anziehen
Frauen. Liebe. Und Sex.
L'arte di Piacere a se Stessi
Mulheres. Amor. E Sexo.
JD Seduzione Assoluta
Перестань быть хорошим мальчиком! Будь плохим мальчиком.
JD Absolute Verführung
JD Sedução Absoluta
Das Leben des charmanten, schamlosen Verführers
Smettila di Fare il Bravo Ragazzo! Essere un Cattivo Ragazzo.
La Vita del Seduttore Affascinante e Spudorato
A Vida do Sedutor Encantador e sem Vergonha
Macho Alfa
Uomo Alfa
Séduction 5.0
Verführung 5.0
Seduzione 5.0
Duro e Senza Vergogna
Duro e Sem Vergonha
L'arte della Durezza
A Arte da Dureza
The Fool's Book
Das Buch der Dummköpfe
Il Libro dei Pazzi
O Livro do Tolo
Dark Seduction
Dunkle Verführung
Sedução Escura
Dark Seduction

Seduzione Oscura
Le livre du fou
Como materializar lo que deseas con el fxxxxxx power
Como materializar o que você quer com o Fxxxxxx Power
El ángel Sex-terminador
El seductor vampiro
O Vampiro Sedutor
Sex-Terminating Angel
The Vampire Seducer
How to Materialize What You Want With The Fxxxxxx Power
El camino del maestro
Il vampiro seduttore
O camiño do mestre

About the Author

Español.

Soy un hombre vividor y divertido que busca el lado bueno de las cosas siempre.

Mi experiencia es el campo de las relaciones personales y de la seducción. Por eso tras dedicarme larguísimas décadas a ello, quiero trasmitir mis conocimientos. Para que las nuevas generaciones tengan unos conceptos que les den una ventaja competitiva sostenible y poderosa en el campo del amor.

Quiero ayudarte a a conseguir tus metas.

Portugués.

Sou um homem animado, e divertido, que sempre procura o lado bom das coisas.

Minha experiência está no campo das relações pessoais e da sedução. É por isso que, após décadas de dedicação a ela, quero transmitir meus conhecimentos.

Quero ajudá-los a alcançar seus objetivos.

Inglés

I am a lively and fun man, who always looks for the good side of things.

My experience is in the field of personal relationships and seduction. That is why, after decades of dedicating myself to it, I want to pass on my knowledge. So that the new generations have concepts that give them a sustainable and powerful competitive advantage in the field of love.

I want to help you achieve your goals

Français Je suis un homme vif et drôle qui cherche toujours le bon côté des choses.

Mon expérience se situe dans le domaine des relations personnelles et de la séduction. C'est pourquoi, après m'y être consacré pendant des décennies, je veux transmettre mes connaissances. Pour que les nouvelles générations disposent de concepts qui leur donnent un avantage concurrentiel durable et puissant dans le domaine de l'amour.

Je veux vous aider à atteindre vos objectifs.